My Life as a Tuskegee Airman

A FIVE DIRECTIONS PRESS BOOK

My Life as a Tuskegee Airman

Hillard Warren Pouncy, Jr.

ISBN-13 978-0615979571
ISBN-10 0615979572

Published in the United States of America by Five Directions Press (www.fivedirectionspress.com).

Book and cover design by Five Directions Press.

Back cover image: B-25 bomber, Courtesy of the U.S. Library of Congress Prints and Photographs Division. Photographed by Mark Sherwood, October 1942. This picture is in the public domain because it was photographed by a naval officer during the regular performance of his duties and is therefore the property of the U.S. government.

Image on last page: Restored P-51 Mustang, with the red tail characteristic of Tuskegee Airmen planes, flown by the Red Tail Project. Photographed by Max Haynes, August 5, 2009, and licensed under a Creative Commons Attribution-Share Alike 3.0 Unported license.

All other photographs are the property of Hillard Warren Pouncy, Jr., and Hillard Warren Pouncy, III.

Five Directions Press logo designed by Colleen Kelley.

FIVE DIRECTIONS PRESS

My name is Dr. Hillard Warren Pouncy, Jr., but you can call me Hill.

I am a Tuskegee Airman. I served my country during World War II because I thought it was the right thing to do. I am proud to have served. When the war ended, I was in training to be a bombardier on a B-25.

I did not always think of myself as a Tuskegee Airman. For most of my adult life, I thought the title belonged only to the men who saw combat. But on March 29, 2007, the airmen as a group received the Congressional Gold Medal, one of the highest civilian honors our country bestows. In 2008, I received a replica of the medal and recognition that I am an official Tuskegee Airman.

My story is a simple one. In everything I did—whether for my country, my family, my people, or my Maker—I did my best. I am convinced this is the meaning of being a Tuskegee Airman. The photos in this book tell that story up to a point.

They cannot tell you how strange I felt the moment World War II ended before I had my chance at combat. They do not tell you of the joy I felt when my grandson graduated from Harvard University. They will not tell you of my grief the day my wife, Mattie, died.

There is only one Congressional Gold Medal for the Tuskegee Airmen, but we all earn the right to a bronze replica. This is mine.

Tuskegee Airman visits students

Contributed photos

Dr. Hillard Pouncy, Jr. spoke with students in fourth and fifth grades at Bright Star Elementary School February 13. Dr. Pouncy shared with students stories from his life, starting from being a Tuskegee Airman during World War II through going to the inauguration of President Barack Obama. He shared an inspirational message with students of never giving up on your dreams no matter how large or impossible they may seem. Below right: Dr. Pouncy shows pictures of his time as a Tuskegee Airmen with the assistance of Bright Star Principal, Mrs. Dale McGill. Above right: Dr. Pouncy shows fifth grade students Kyle Kelly and Shelby Walker his replica of the Tuskegee Airmen's Medal of Honor.

I began telling my story of being a Tuskegee Airman to my grandson's class at the Swarthmore Rutledge Elementary School. Now I tell it several times a month in Atlanta, GA.

I entered service as a
young man …

and became a major
in the Air Force
Reserve.

Military Service

I was a student at Tuskegee Institute, and my best student was Mattie Mae Hunter. She became my wife in 1947. We had a son after we were married, and we named him Hillard Warren Pouncy III.

I later earned a Ph.D. in organic chemistry from Syracuse University. I worked for many years as a chemist for Union Carbide Corporation and was co-participant on one patent.

My father was a minister and presiding elder in the African Methodist Episcopal Church. His name—Hilliard Warren Pouncy.

My grandson works in the computer industry. His name—Hillard Thomas Pouncy.

Tuskegee Airmen

The Tuskegee Airmen were the first black combat pilots to serve for the United States armed forces. They came from all over the country to try out for the first ever experiment to train black pilots at Tuskegee Air Field in Alabama. As members of the 332nd Fighter Group, they not only had to face the daily challenges that came from serving in the battlefield, but they had to overcome racism from other pilots and those who were determined not to give them respect as soldiers. They had to struggle against a history of racism practiced by the armed forces that refused to give blacks the same recognition for their service that they would have given whites. The armed forces believed that blacks lacked the intelligence needed for combat and that they performed better in menial jobs rather than in the battlefield.

From L to R: Eugene Henry, Hill Pouncy, Dr. Jemison, Val Archer, Wilbur Mason, Travon Dennis

Dr. Mae Jemison & Atlanta Chapter Tuskegee Airmen

When I was a younger man, I believed in a world well captured in Thomas Wolfe's book *The Right Stuff*. I believed that some of us have the right stuff, and most of us do not. Life, I believed, was a series of tests that we either passed or failed on our way to learning whether we had the right stuff or not. One failure, and our fate was sealed.

The lesson I have learned as a Tuskegee Airman is that life can also be a matter of learning whether our stuff is right. Whether we persevere and how we conduct ourselves in the face of trials, especially those that we fail. I believe the Tuskegee Airmen taught me that my stuff is right. I believe they taught my country that my people's stuff is right.

About this book

Thank you, Gudmund Iversen, for the encouragement and Photoshopping.

Thanks to my son, Hillard Pouncy, for editorial help.

Thanks to the Atlanta Chapter of the Airmen's Association for fellowship and assistance.

Made in the USA
Lexington, KY
19 April 2017